Milet Publishing
Smallfields Cottage, Cox Green
Rudgwick, Horsham, West Sussex
RH12 3DE England
info@milet.com
www.milet.com
www.milet.co.uk

First English–German edition published by Milet Publishing in 2013

Copyright © Milet Publishing, 2013

ISBN 978 1 84059 841 4

Original Turkish text written by Erdem Seçmen
Translated to English by Alvin Parmar and adapted by Milet

Illustrated by Chris Dittopoulos
Designed by Christangelos Seferiadis

Printed and bound in Turkey by Ertem Matbaası

My Bilingual Book

Touch
Das Tasten

English–German

Milet

How do you know what's smooth or rough?

Wie kannst Du wissen, ist es glatt oder rau?

Your hands are your sensors, they're sensitive and tough!

Deine Hände sind Sensoren, empfindlich und schlau!

If you play without gloves in the snow,

Spielst Du im Winter ohne Handschuhe im Schnee,

your hands will get cold, you know!

werden Deine Hände ganz kalt, ojemine!

Teddy bear feels soft and furry.

Teddybären sind weich und pelzig,

Play-dough feels nicely squishy!

Spielknete ist angenehm wabbelig.

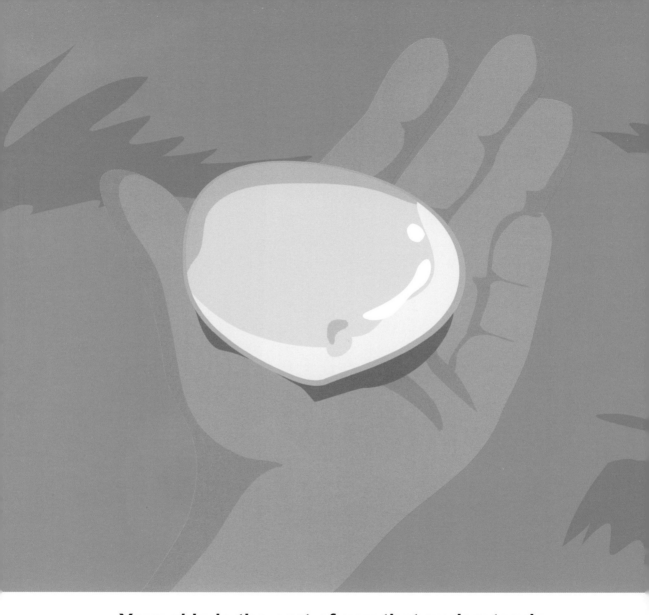

Your skin is the part of you that understands

Deine Haut ist der Teil von Dir, der hilft zu erkennen,

how different things feel in your hands.

wie verschiedene Dinge sich anfühlen in Deinen Händen.

The touch sense comes from nerves in your skin

Der Tastsinn funktioniert über die Nerven in der Haut,

that travel to your brain and say, message in!

die ans Gehirn weiterleiten, Berührung aufgebaut!

Your brain decides quickly what to do

Dein Hirn entscheidet blitzschnell, was ist zu tun

and nerves send the message back to you!

und über Nerven erhältst Du die Antwort im Nu!

So when you touch something sharp,

Wenn Du also etwas Scharfes berührst

your nerves tell you, stop!

melden Deine Nerven Dir "Stopp", dass du damit aufhörst!

Or they tell you to be gentle

Oder Sie geben Dir Signale, sanft zu sein,

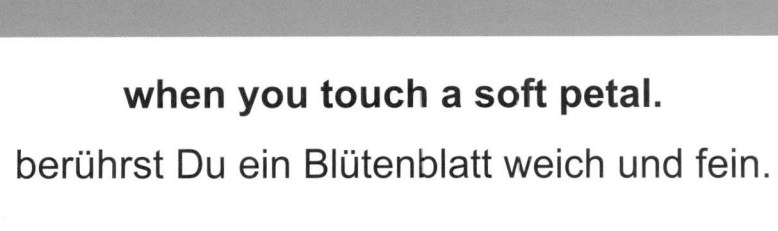

when you touch a soft petal.

berührst Du ein Blütenblatt weich und fein.

Touch helps you learn about nature and things.

Das Tasten hilft Dir, mehr über Natur und Dinge zu erfahren.

It's really amazing, all the knowledge it brings!

Es ist einfach erstaunlich, wie viel Informationen wir dadurch haben!

Your touch can also show you care,

Eine Berührung kann auch zeigen, wie sehr Du Dich sorgst,

like hugging someone who is dear.

wenn Du jemanden knuddelst, den Du sehr magst.